A Boat Called *Annalise*

For my son Kim at Brighton
For my daughter Berith at Aberystwyth

Think of the long trip home.
Should we have stayed at home and thought of here?
Where should we be today?

Elizabeth Bishop

And in loving memory of Dannie Abse

A Boat Called *Annalise*

Lynne Hjelmgaard

Seren is the book imprint of
Poetry Wales Press Ltd.
57 Nolton Street, Bridgend, Wales, CF31 3AE
www.serenbooks.com
facebook.com/SerenBooks
twitter@SerenBooks

The right of Lynne Hjelmgaard to be identified as
the author of this work has been asserted in accordance
with the Copyright, Designs and Patents Act, 1988.

ISBN: 978-1-78172-310-4
ebook: 978-1-78172-312-8
Kindle: 978-1-78172-313-5

A CIP record for this title is available from the British Library.

The publisher acknowledges the financial assistance of the Welsh Books Council.

Cover Artwork: Ink Drawing by Jan Petersen

Printed in Bembo by Bell & Bain Ltd, Glasgow.

Contents

I   That Feeling of Boat

II   On Shore

III   Elsewhere

IV   A Brief Return to the Tropics

I

That Feeling of Boat

You must take up your well-shaped oar and go on a journey until you come where there are men living who know nothing of the sea.

from *The Odyssey, Book XI*

Navigation

I.M. of Stig

1

I captured
your silhouette floating
in an aura of blues one
hand in your pocket one
hand for the ship you
steered with your foot
on the wheel wearing
a straw hat like a cowboy.

You liked to handle heavy rope
could splice a line
could walk a heeling deck.
The sun baked our backs
after island's rain washed
salt from our bodies.

Martha the autopilot hummed.

2

You left in a hurry
sextant on the table
pointers spread on the chart.
The cabin door open –
now still swinging back and forth
forth and back.

Put on your old blue jacket.
I'll even let you stuff your pipe
if you promise to plot a course
to the exact position
of where you are.

That Feeling of Boat

(the beginning of the journey)

Wind hollers through the ship's rigging –
heavy lines hammer it.

My husband struggles with the lights
at the top of the mast.

(The booming start of the diesel,
odorous fumes and thunder overhead.

The commotion of unpacking sails,
snapping like Christmas crackers.

The quiet reprieve when they are hoisted
and we've passed the last buoy.

The release of being underway,
heading for the unknown.)

The sea draws us to her,
each swell a journey opening.

Who are we looking for?
What did we leave behind?

I doze trance-like, or jolt awake
unsettled in a half dream.

My husband adjusts the jib sheet,
cranks the winch tight, and tighter.

Annalise leans over on her side,
closed-hauled flat and drawing.

When land disappears my senses sharpen –
necessity replaces worry.

Is there sorrow here?
Will I become less afraid?

I listen to the wash of waves,

wash   of   waves.

There is a thick
anxious kind of jittery.

Up down rolling is good cure.

Away from civilization
we'll keep becoming capable.

(Aren't you afraid in a storm?)

Outside each propelling constellation
but inside that feeling of boat.

It demands and bruises,
cuts pride, hardens stomachs.

I'm reminded of purpose,
aroused by briny smells.

We confide and trust in twenty tons,
talk to it, nurture it,

give in, get back,
she lulls me to sleep   lulls   me   to   sleep.

In evenings there will be Venus and
in mornings there will be a sea freshened moon.

Seamanship

Lie in your bunk
with a bucket beside you.
Hold on to it,
it can slide away.
Eat (if you can).

If a sea cock breaks
and the engine room floods
and the bilge pumps jam,
don't worry.
You can fix it.

Even if you smell of diesel
and are too tired to hand-steer,
too hungry for breakfast
and homesick for gardens and trees,
keep your watch.

Wedge yourself in berth
wiggling and wretched.
Doze.
Wake up
with an urge to get there.

Don't hold any grudges.
What other way is there
to handle life at sea?

Nowhere else to go.
Daylight less than an hour away.

★

Flying fish squirm on the bow
and are scooped back through the scuppers
as it submerges and ploughs,

submerges and ploughs.
One hand for the ship!

Like mice-men our feet pedal
inside a perpetual wheel.
Plankton, fellow wanderer,
twirls and sways.

And there's no turning back;
nor can the bird blown offshore,
now clinging momentarily to our rail.

Later, on a clear and windless day
we lazy about, enjoy our breakfast
do a spring clean below.

In the music of wind and water,
our bodies shift to a living-on-land mode
and forget, for a few hours

or days even, who and where we are.
We have free run about the cabin,
no lurching for grab-holds or
struggles with a sloping loo.

Our spirits lift and open
as we glare at our reflections
in the smooth surface azure.

They look back at us knowingly.

Connected to the universe,
disconnected from the world.

Novice

Annalise ploughs through the wind's eye,
beating in a blow.
The mast vibrates, sails flutter
until settled or are tightened
to lie flat. Once more lines snap,
shrouds hum, and the hull leans over
as waves water the deck or us.

After all this
Annalise is in the same exact spot.
Foul weather gear
is too heavy to wear;
and even worse to shed it
if one dared to go below.
(The wretched lurching up and down.)

This is a washing machine.
I am turned inside out.
My husband can crawl on deck
while seas wash over him,
take sails down,
mend them
when they tear,
repair the engine, the rigging, the head
and, at the same time, cook.

I stare at my own fear-shadow
for what feels like days upon days
until I realize I still exist;
the seas are endurable
my nausea has disappeared.

My husband knows I will come around,
be counted on for my night-watch,
report anything suspect.

But soon we'll be edging closer,
I feel it.
The more difficult
to reach, the stronger
the sense and
longing for land.

The moon rises a bold yellow
as if the night suddenly lifts a heavy curtain.
Dawn brings a swell drumming us closer
on to a more turbulent ridge.

Out from under comes a large fin.
It thrashes then plunges.
At that moment fever rises in my throat.
I was twelve days a christened sailor!

How precious a thing
to lie steady,
snug and warm,
to know the pleasure of
a small island
with a spit of sand
to wake you
by its mere presence.

A Bucket of Carrots

for Stig

Cabbage, fried, boiled or stewed, is a tasty dish
and its worth on a boat with a small holding tank
need not be questioned.

Pick up a scraper,
splash your fingers in salty water
and peel carrots.

It's Vitamin A.
Good for your eyesight.

I give you food.
I give you love.

Don't eat any before
I've mixed them with
the cabbage and garlic
we bought in San Salvador.

There is something more
in a bucket of carrots
or in a puff of air
filled with an aroma

of salty peels
scattered onto
a piece of Dacron cloth.

Night Watch

A freighter dances over the water:
a large, tubby ballerina
gracefully tiptoeing on a wire,
waving as she tilts and bends.

She's a star beneath the rocking stars.
She's a toy, a flimsy teacup
in boiling stew for the sea-beast.

We are in the Ocean's mouth,
territory unknown,
waves speak as if to say:

we too long for the smell
and comfort of land
but want to leave once it's tasted.

I hear the slush of the ship's wake,
smell the tar on deck,
the exhaust of diesel.

She carries a heavy load
beneath her waterline.
First a flash of red light,
then a flash of sloping green.

Over and back, back and over,
we won't collide.
She's a mile away.

But I fight to stay awake –
and for a few seconds tremble,
having lost sight of
the freighter's hypnotic dance.

Wind speed rises,
the barometer drops.
Clouds loom, stars
and moon disappear.

Then *Annalise* falls off a wave,
and falls and rises and falls
into a rogue sea.

We hurry to shorten sail,
stumble over lines
clear the decks

rehearse in our minds
the worst scene:
abandon ship!

Our darker selves
tense up and question:
Is this why we've come?

I think of how Peregrine's crew
were last seen
hanging onto wreckage....

Land, its pleasantries
that much stronger.
Like the fruit

on the tree Tantalus
could never grasp.
I long for lights

on the shoreline,
old friends that appear
and disappear.

We are machinery and
cargo amid seaweed
and sharks.

We are tightrope dancers –
no net below.
We kept our day watch

now our dogwatch.
Is that a white light ahead?
It doesn't move.

'So uncertain a thing'
Columbus must have thought.
He did not wish to declare
that it was land.

The no-moon night,
the dark ghostly creatures,
the slow-motion small tsunamis

engulf *Annalise*,
reek of rotten seaweed,
spilled oil, dead shark.

Through Binoculars I See a Turquoise Harbour

I knew how to carve a coconut
halve it, quarter it,
drink the milk,
eat the meat,

to take a sail down to the bottom of a full moon bay
or walk across a mountain at dawn.
That pastel village lining the coast
was better off before we got there.
The sheep still wandered that West End alone.

I loved island life.
Some days working, other days not.
As long as you're making enough
nobody seemed to care – nothing.
That was '85.

Now I dream on
setting our anchor down
for some more piece of that lazy.
Through binoculars I view
Jim's pink house dripping of thunderstorm;
his children in uniforms running around.

I know that smell of tangy-flavoured soil
and the mongoose mud path
straight up to the top hills, fresher and
higher than those with whining sheep
looking down on
sails and sand and coral heads.

Jumping out at me –
the more bluer than blue –
with white caps foaming
the whole way across
to Soper's Hole.

II

On Shore

The Return

We anchor and can't wait
to taste it again. Slowly

it becomes familiar,
becomes love,

brings us
out of ourselves.

Lushness and green, mule scent
mongoose and wet mud,

palms more pungent
and savoury, the damp night:

its feminine foliage,
its woolly pointed hills.

Tango nights and couples
promenading under the stars.

We fell asleep with the roosters,
the waves, rumblings in the bay.

Palm trees rustle when
they know the rain is coming.

A stick on the wall can fly.
A cockroach big as a crunchy bird.

It's so bright I can read without glasses,
see for long distances,

listening to water, drinking water,
waiting for water.

The whole day floats
away with water.

I relish the sun
worship it,

sit in it, starve for it,

burn for it.

On Shore

You phone.
Your voice sounds rested
as it never is anywhere else.
I imagine you settled in the dark companionway.
The cabin's warm, sticky,
you've already studied the chart,
counted the miles to the Canaries
with your pointers.
I feel their edges
not far from your lustful eyes on me.

Still *Annalise* has that smell: slightly honeyed,
rusty cans, soapy rags, brewed coffee,
whole cinnamon in a drawer.

Below, the eye meets wide and mellowed wood,
rounded doors and narrow recesses.
People have asked, 'That space
how can one live or sleep or...?'
I always say there's more
(more than anywhere)
even when our bodies brush
just miss by moments in passing.

I watched the hanging lantern move – forth   back
as the hanging basket moved – forth   back
your reflection off the mast,
sandpaper in a bag, varnish and sponges,
brushes and gloves.

You've rubbed the compass on the wheel
to silk – placid and lingering.
Annalise has brought us safely
into this other world
like both our mothers gone.

Jim

You think I work here all the time, mon?
Want to get away, get the hell away.

West Indian pidgin sings to me, they work the hotels, the ferries, the taxis.

Sometimes mon, they put their anchor down and forget to tie it on board.
They can't get the engine started so they bang into other boats.

'Go for it honey', the girl honeymooner had said
as we snorkelled in Honeymoon Bay.
She forgot to remove her jewellery or did I forget to tell her?
The current is strong, it pushes quickly, it will not be easy on the way back.

They drag a line in the water it gets caught in the screws mon,
while everyone sits around gettin' tan. They run on the rocks 'cause
they can't find the channel.

'Protect and nurture our children, they are dark and mellow as their soil,'
said the Chief Minister of Our Affairs.

Don't worry about this harbour, mon.
Just leave when the lighting's good.

He sashays away and disappears
behind the shack.

Trade wind, daydream,
a pelican dives for fish.
Another pelican is the only one watching.

The Thief

The pearly-eyed thrasher steals crumbs
of Special K or bullies a melon.

His skittish mate sneaks inside – hopping from chair
to floor – licking the dead mosquitoes, no-see-uhms.

Tough, he circles the terrace then sits on his perch –
the tallest branch of the papaya tree,

closest to the porch; pretends to clean himself
while enjoying an excellent view.

He stretches his neck, I bite a piece of toast.
He nips a feather, I think of peck marks

on the screen upstairs, more visible,
more piercing in the morning sun.

He thrashes the territory with high-pitched notes,
then lands defiantly on my end of the table.

I'm cornered, too face-to-face, I cower and flee.
This dagger-beak bird-head spies my every move.

Only the two of us.

Goldfish in a pond, hot bird-breath in pursuit,
my bare neck and arms, his daring wings.

Island Gossip

We heard there is a born-again Pastor converting single mothers
on the main island.
We heard white man gets the label still, *white man.*
We heard the workers haven't gotten a raise in years.
We heard the whites and blacks live together so far but you never know.
We heard the man who owns the fancy restaurant on the main island
is into wife swapping.
We heard pirates used to hide here with their women. (They still do.)
We heard a woman checked into the resort for two weeks, paid her bill
in advance and took an overdose of pills.
We heard the cigarette boats make drug runs to Venezuela.
We heard about a troubled hermit who people rarely see.
We heard it takes the rest of a lifetime to find the way out.

The Ferry Called *When*

Jim drove me to the harbour
through the back of town.

The shacks were not bright pink and blue,
like those along the waterfront.

Sick brown, dark beige.
The palm trees didn't look too healthy either.

We passed broken-down cars, truck parts,
scraggy bushes in need of nourishment.

A growling anorexic dog, menacing as Cerberus,
was tied to a post where the junkies used to hang out.

He got loose, chased us to the water's edge.
'Ignore the dog, don't say a thing,' Jim said.

Across the bight the mainland disappeared
behind a white and ancient mist.

The green at the spit of its tongue grew dark and pointed.
The mist, Lethe-like, disappeared, its mouth opened.

There was a gust of wind, a pelican on a rock.
The snarling dog exposed his teeth, stood guard.

I believed in Jim, got out of the car.
The air smelt of coconut, wet wood, tropical rain.

Nobody knows what time the ferry comes.
That's why they call it *When*.

The Burning Tree

Where it will stand until it falls down decorated with flowers.
Where the families line up on the side of the road in their town clothes:
    men in shirts, ties and jackets, women in straw hats and long dresses.
Where the mother tries to comfort her remaining son.
Where the grandson tries to comfort the grandmother.
Where no one should have to suffer so.
Where we saw the smoke trail on top of the mountain and we thought they
were burning garbage again or we thought it was the freighter that ran
    aground again.
Where they've blocked the road and no more cars are coming.
Where the swaggering police tell all the cars to turn around.
Where you take the long road up the steeps instead of the long curvy flat road
    along the coast where they drive too fast.
Where further out the water becomes turquoise becomes green and the blue
    turns into shadows that move up the hill and the patterns fly downwards
    to touch the reef to touch the grieving families by the side of the road.
Where they make their graves above the ground like small huts
    covered with wreaths of yellow, blue and pink carnations.
Where the pelicans circle closer to the place where the men were shot
    in their car under the burning tree.

Jim's Coconut Rat

*We, the local fisherman, ferry owners, pleasure boat owners
and sea lovers of the 3rd District ask the Government to
preserve and maintain the mangroves. We are being chased
out of the grove.*

The tourist is on the make:
He's a rat a clown an imposter,
is in love with icons,
is in love with gossip,
is at times a burden,
is slippery,
is close enough to swallow your smell,
is never whole,
shops his way,
using up the world,
going everywhere,
getting away,
disappearing,
coming back for more.

*White men in the sun,
dark men in the shade.*

How they stand up in yachts.
How we stand up in trucks.

Watch us hose down the decks.
Watch us load their beer and chips.

Watch us take their garbage.
Watch us crawl up the mast.

Watch us scrub the boats.
Watch us bring the ice.

They come with the cruise ships
but they are not the spenders.

Sure, the government gets the tax
and the taxis get the rides.

White men in the sun,
dark men in the shade.

Leaving Port

We need the music of wind and water,
the horizon our home.

We sand and rub *Annalise* with oil and wax,
fill her with fresh food and tins,

blankets and clothes, special
sea-going non-skid bowls.

There are many problems with engine
or pump. Lists and more lists:

grind a propeller or rotting wood,
clean the bronze and study the charts.

But for now, we rest at anchor.

They are singing and singing
in the Baptist Church.

Wind slurping dinghy in the water
puts us to sleep.

Flag flutter, clang of the rigging,
engine now quiet, puts us to sleep.

We wake to houses in the shipyard,
old ferry at the dock,

channel markers, yachts, speedboats,
the pink house on the hill.

Our friend Jim waves to us where mango trees
shade the water's edge

and pelicans gather and
dive for fish.

A donkey and baby chicks
hang around the shops.

Annalise has shown us waves
as tall as New York

and brain coral and conch
on a deserted beach.

She fills us with newness,
we give away our old.

We need the music of wind and water,
the horizon our home.

One hand for strength, the other for light.

III

Elsewhere

Crisscross

(France)

The voyage is a past you needed
to catch up with, a congruent line.

The months since the journey moved
in their own latitudes and longitudes

crisscrossed with colour and weather
to harden your face.

A storm: you stayed in the middle of things
I headed for the bunk.

I remember waves like fountains etched on paper.
We rounded the point longing for harbour.

The blue wind, the biting spray.
The relentless sea shoving us from side to side.

Still you thrived in an ocean's wild night
and spiked your coffee with too much rum.

Now the problems arrive post-Atlantic
and must be solved onshore.

You blame the both of you:
the one with the mad eyes and briefcase
the other for the sea story he holds.

A Boat Called Annalise

Two people together for so long can be rekindled at sea
and it changes me – (if alone one would be searching for a mate,
if one had a mate one would be worrying about being alone).
　　　　　He is my crimson thread.

I remember sky thickening and thinning
between gratifying moments
and wisps of purple cloud
　　　　　going right through and down.

My husband is often intent on leaving no matter what the weather;
I have different thoughts at millennium speed but
could only choose one course through that maze:
　　　　　relationship's laborious track.

And though I know his most intimate morning habits: bathing routine,
first coffee, cigarette, water on face, shave, shower,
second cup while organizing papers,
　　　　　we've become ordinary –

drifters/sailors settling down for cash. This is like the end of the nineties
with Money Exchange International, more Euro dollars for us
not the Asians/Africans,
last night he said:
　　　　　'Why do you look at me like I'm a stranger?'

The taxi driver who drove us through the city was very kind
and Moroccan, likes to visit the wilderness of Montana,
Oregon, Quebec. A gentle surge in the harbour made its way
　　　　　through the canal.

Back at the hotel, having to decide between the le/la in French
and et/en in Danish, Jean Pablo tries to impress the girl who
went topless in Manhattan.
They are his associates now:

mobile phones, laptops, free drinks around the bar;
running pool water sounds like Coney Island in the 70s.
Then we'd take the subway to the last stop with
soggy tuna, wet plums.

Sometimes I hesitate on the edge
of his mathematical energy: hard-driving
industry, telecom, facts.

Male to female – join my world, I'll join yours.
He needles me, I needle him on weight gain and health.
Is being at sea better than
cooking and writing on Sundays?

He left this morning at 6 am wearing his light blue suit,
has lots to do with meetings and lunch at Hotel George V,
smoking, high blood pressure, no exercise.
He laughed when

I said, 'That was five-minute sex. I want as much time as one of your lousy
presentations.' They are concrete and functional,
mine are flowing, indefinite.
A chapter of what he would be like if we'd never met.

Directions

I travel South by French rail to visit our sailboat *Annalise*.
(We sail with her when we can then leave her in a good harbour,
returning when we can.)
A young couple embrace on the seat next to me.
He plays with their fingers, her hands and ring.

I think of you and me and see you bathed
in sea-light and wooden shadows.
Your face is tough and itchy.
You scratch your head.
Your sounds and smells flow freely
between *Annalise's* planks.
They are different than they used to be.
Now they are: stale tobacco, scuzzy in the morning,
phlegm and coughing that I can't stand to hear.
Your occasional hard-breathing voice is on the phone
full of harsh tones as you fend off and make your way
in the world of voicemail.

I feel a pulling in my stomach.
I see your boss's ugly face on the other side of the globe
telling you worldly telecom nonsense.
You try to make sense of it
and I try to make sense of you telling,
'Tomorrow night I leave at 8 get in at 9 arrive at 10.'

I am happy that your children love you.
One just left yesterday with his sweetheart.
I miss him a lot.
The older one is around for a while.
She needs us a lot.
I feel a change between you and me.

I watch an airplane pass overhead.
It sounds close.
Too close.

Then I go back to how it was.
I dream of you on top of a sail-bag on deck
and me on top of you in layers.
Lamp oil burning below.
Anchor chain scuffing the bottom.
Musty scents of the bilge on our bodies and clothes.
No one – nothing else.

Apartment 5F

I take soundings through this Copenhagen window.
The grey cat, in the room across the way,

follows sparrows through the glass,
his fat head ping-pongs from side to side.

I see you in the kitchen stuffing your pipe,
hear your slippers shuffle on the wooden floor.

Those last days you couldn't lift your feet, the thinness
of your body, your incomprehensible state.

Where did you sleep,
where did I?

During night watch on *Annalise*
I used to search for buoys,

the channel, a point of return.
Sometimes in foul weather

when safely below, I'd tell myself:
no gale rages above!

(Though the signs of malady were everywhere,
this one raged in you.)

When the dying bird landed
on our ship we still tried

to feed it life. There are species
that cannot survive alone,

that can only move through water
if pushed by winds, currents, tides.

Before death you saw *Annalise*
from an unfathomable distance.
Wherever she is moored now, you are there.

I gravitate North, towards her,
like the beacons I used to steer for.

Ape's Love Song

(Copenhagen)

1–

It's 6 am.
The long echo of his night-full *o*
works its way to the likes of *ah*.

He swings from a pole with outstretched arms
and later gently strokes the head

of the beloved in his lap. The zoo–park's tenor
examines his and hers.

The highest bar *I'll miss you*
'til I'm gone

opens the throat
from the depths of his ape belly

and when Spring birds begin again
beside the tree's cryptic carving

on the bark
a lost Jane.

2-

I lie in bed (almost a mile away)
and hear the ape's melodious song.

A furry, fiery ball of breath
singing to his beloved.

It ricochets off concrete walls,
it somersaults in bicycle-laden,
tulip-growing courtyards.

His arms are outstretched, her lips are thick.
Love penetrates glass.

As in a tender dream I too was wooed
with *a happiness that was simply true.*

It is Danish mid-summer.
At 7 am the moon slowly fades.

Roots

(Roervig bay, the path beneath our old house)

The last birch tree is dying. The others and you
I also grieve for, their root system destroyed,
mere stumps. In Jan's painting,

though outlined as silhouettes,
they are alive again. They do not falter;
my eyes catch them, move with them.

There are restless Danish skies, pale and airy.
Our two figures in the landscape,
where nothing changes and
everything has: trees, friendship, love.

Jan and I are no longer close.
Yet with you I am infinitely linked
to the place, to Jan, to the baseline
of its trees, to the root system destroyed.

Nomad Song

Now, far from the sea
the sea-lure remains.
Come home, I say.

My hands can carry less and less.
I want you near,
but you move further away.

Your belongings come along:
a small teak stamp box,
smooth and soft in my hands.

A tiny glass hexagon
colourful parrots inside.
They swing with you in eternity
on little plastic vines.

Chatwin's *Anatomy of Restlessness*,
the last book you read.
'We are travellers from birth.'

You, too, shed things and places
like layers of skin.

Now, far from the sea
the sea-lure remains.

Come home, I say,
but you move further away.

Four Walls

I now have four walls to form and shape:
and note each night what the day has brought,
and note each day where the night has travelled.

I surrender to this place
and this place will house me
until I'm compelled to leave.

Columbus ventured out and
discovered the sad relief of departure.

The excitement in the sound
of water breaking on shore,
foreign hilltops peaking through the mist,
waiting to be sun-befriended.

Other men too searched for imaginary islands,
disappearing coasts, longing to be refreshed
by newness. The danger of it.

Landfalls filled their dreams,
though they could at times
sing to the uplifting swell.

Sea journeys have taught me
steadiness, to be more sure
but here, now that I am back
will I be able?

London 2012-13

Rhea Americana in Golders Hill Park

Bewildered and feathered,
                    moist with dew, captured
in the headlights of the morning sun.

Your beak drips spittle
                    down your question-mark neck.
Puddle eyes stare on either side
                    of your tiny timid head.

Am I a blur or a halo
                    in your blue-green bird zone,
or a fuzzed-out figure
                    dithery in the wind?

Every night you too must face
                    dark London alone.
The owls seem used to solitude,
                    the deer have each other.

In the afternoon you disappeared,
                    until later I found you,
hidden behind a bush,
                    staring blankly into air like a statue.

Now you squat forlorn
                    and droopy, your ballroom plumage sinks
into the mud where bravely,
                    moments ago, you hugged the fence.

Both of us may be flightless,
                    but our wings can spread
and sail when we run.

White Clover

For Dannie

We, childlike in our trust, cover the grasslands
where we find ourselves
and spread.
                       Our roots endure, keep each other.

Heartened to fall asleep
to the sound of rain,
                       we dream of bees, we whisper,
deep in summer,
hold close.

We are clusters of tender heads, fragile
with sighs, mishaps, concerns;
rounded tips and lashes,
                       meadow scent mild and
mothering.

                       Bees.

Love me, love me not, love me.

                       The bees.

Our honey within, thickening.

Our trefoil leaves calling out:
I'm the one, choose me.

Your Pen Rushes to My Hand

Your pen rushes to my hand
like your warm hands used to,

are you sending me lines
to last for eternity? Once again

I'm compelled to scribble on paper
as I stand outside your house.

On the wet London street
puddles gather in shadowy places:

just in front of the black gate, beneath
the first step, next to the green door

with the bell that doesn't work
and the old falling-apart mat.

Places where water accumulates
having nowhere else to go.

Doors and windows are locked,
curtains are drawn. Hedges tower above

more pointed, more heaven-reaching,
encircle the house like a tomb. Now

they keep out the light. During your last years
(and days) you filled me up with all the light

you could. Afraid, I've been preparing
since we met....

Like always when I leave I still see
you stand at the front door waving

and I wave while walking
until the top of your head disappears.

IV

A Brief Return to the Tropics

Return to the Tropics

I sit childlike at the edge of the cliff,
and hear my name chanted by geckos
when I close my eyes.

The mountain on the tropical coast,
in silhouette (the moon rises just behind it),
no longer knows its way to me.

Still, the island has a pointed rock-shape
like the head of a lizard; there is a ruin now
where there used to be lights.

A cactus has died, its thick-skinned
shadow more obtuse and creature-like
in the star-shine.

The tamarind have all but disappeared.
Trade winds occupy our house on the hill:
they blow me in – they blow me out.

But I longed to get back.

Midnight howling gales
clear the way for morning,
summon the new.

Waves no longer operate in threes:
break on the rocks,
die down, start up.

I remember local men
fishing in a small boat
seemingly buried in a swell.

They'd disappear, then rise up again,
yell excitedly to *Annalise* higher
on the top of a foamy green crest.

Their boat appeared
out of nowhere
the way geckos do.

On land the men's gait
is laboured and slow.
Though I know them
they pass me blankly.

But still I want *back*.

Threads of black clouds
seem to tease the moon
off its axis.

I close my eyes, dream,
it drifts and spins aimlessly,
shows its never-before-seen side.

Morning at Sea

Many Marys (Virgin Islands)

I remember at dawn,
after twelve days at sea,
we took a long tack offshore
to approach the islands
from the best angle
so we could glide our way
between them.

Volcanic peaks welcomed us,
their jagged slopes shifted
to a blue only a shade darker
than the sky-dyed sea.

The shoreline unfolded
as we entered the lagoon
heading for a horseshoe beach
*'where all ships of Spain
could lie and be safe'.*

Wind funnelled down through the hills.
Annalise's stern swung in the rippling tide.
And in the land's lee we anchored
behind a hissing, coral reef.

Tierra! We could not get there fast enough.
Our sea-legs trembled. A cock crowed.

Here Europeans discovered cannibals.
There was a mysterious odour of cloves
and orchids, a discomforting cry.

*Who were we looking for?
What did we leave behind?*

On the beach blackened remnants of a feast.

Connections

Yachts are tied to wooden pilings,
(patient in their tortured movement)
they lean, bow and rise, lean, bow and rise.

Dock lines twist and stretch
(forgiving and strong, tightened
to the maximum).

A captain rubs the hull
of his enormous yacht – smooth to shine.
(Methodically, in no hurry.)

As you and I had once rubbed
our smaller *Annalise's* hull – smooth to shine.
(Methodically, in no hurry.)

Clumsy, I step aboard a friend's yacht,
afraid to tumble. Instantly I sense
the distance travelled, know this space.

The thrill of sails and hull that work
with water and wind. My upturned
face in the happiness, its salty smell.

Or a night sail under the Milky Way,
taken in by rawness, the immediacy
of the unknown, an embrace.

But then, uneasy again, disconnected.
I lie in this strange bunk, surrender to the motion,
the clatter, the groans, rattles and thumps.

This rock-and-roll.
This bull with a harness on,
tamed by cowboy wind.

Postscript: Because of the Beauty of the Ship Herself

When we found her
it happened quickly,
when we left her
it felt like a divorce.

We had worked our way into *Annalise*:
the pungent smell of her deep shadowy bilge;
dawn-walks to showers
in mouldy leather shoes.

(Wet on the trip in
wet on the trip out.)

Annalise peeled away
layers of ourselves.
Old meandering patterns
shed like unwanted winter clothes.

We learned to care
for her bronze, steel and wood,
devotedly washed and rubbed
all her curves and corners.

Her decks cracked and creaked,
rigging throbbed and hummed,
sails fluttered and snapped,
hull pounded and leapt,

the booming sea-roar crouching to pounce
until *Annalise* lifted her heavy rounded stern
in the very last unbalanced moment
and reduced seawater to slush.

In harbour, ships' wakes and rolls
rocked us, sleepily secure,
water gurgled under her hull
like gentle, shaking bells.
We slept 'til she opened our ears
to all natural sounds.

Our ship made music.
Our ship was music.

Acknowledgements

Acknowledgements are owed to the editors of the following publications where these poems, or earlier versions of these poems, first appeared:

Acumen, Bombay Gin (USA), Dispatch Detroit (USA) Fire, Leviathan Quarterly, Loop 3 Press 62 (USA) Pharos, Poetry Salzburg Review, Poetry Wales, Shearsman Magazine, Tears in the Fence, The Rialto and *The Warwick Review*.

'White Clover' was commissioned for a wildflower anthology. (Editor/Artist Clare Whistler). It was performed at the Small World Theatre in Cardigan, Wales, 2015.

Some of the poems, in earlier versions, appeared in the pamphlet *Distance Through the Water* (I Want Press, France).

Some lines in 'Morning at Sea' were taken from and inspired by reading *Admiral of the Ocean Sea – A life of Christopher Columbus*.

I would like to thank Douglas Oliver, Alice Notley and friends in Paris who first read these poems; Wendy French, Mimi Khalvati and her groups in Lewes and London for their feedback and generous responses; Jan Petersen of Copenhagen who made the drawing for the cover design.

I would especially like to thank Dannie Abse for his love, encouragement, support and guidance.

My warm thanks to my editor Amy Wack for her help and encouragement.

And thanks to my children for acquiring their 'sea legs'; for their patience, love and ability to endure.

Also by the Author

Distance Through the Water (I Want Press, France, 2002)

Manhattan Sonnets (Redbeck Press, 2003)

The Ring (Shearsman Books, 2011)

SEREN

Well chosen words

Seren is an independent publisher with a wide-ranging list which includes poetry, fiction, biography, art, translation, criticism and history. Many of our books and authors have been on longlists and shortlists for – or won – major literary prizes, among them the Costa Award, the Jerwood Fiction Uncovered Prize, the Man Booker, the Desmond Elliott Prize, The Writers' Guild Award, Forward Prize and TS Eliot Prize.

At the heart of our list is a good story told well or an idea or history presented interestingly or provocatively. We're international in authorship and readership though our roots are here in Wales (Seren means Star in Welsh), where we prove that writers from a small country with an intricate culture have a worldwide relevance.

Our aim is to publish work of the highest literary and artistic merit that also succeeds commercially in a competitive, fast changing environment. You can help us achieve this goal by reading more of our books – available from all good bookshops and increasingly as e-books. You can also buy them at 20% discount from our website, and get monthly updates about forthcoming titles, readings, launches and other news about Seren and the authors we publish.

www.serenbooks.com